Dear Parents and Educators,

Welcome to Penguin Young Readers! As parents and educators, you know that each child develops at his or her own pace—in terms of speech, critical thinking, and, of course, reading. Penguin Young Readers recognizes this fact. As a result, each Penguin Young Readers book is assigned a traditional easy-to-read level (1–4) as well as a Guided Reading Level (A–P). Both of these systems will help you choose the right book for your child. Please refer to the back of each book for specific leveling information. Penguin Young Readers features esteemed authors and illustrators, stories about favorite characters, fascinating nonfiction, and more!

Daring Amelia

LEVEL **3**

GUIDED READING LEVEL **L**

This book is perfect for a **Transitional Reader** who:
- can read multisyllable and compound words;
- can read words with prefixes and suffixes;
- is able to identify story elements (beginning, middle, end, plot, setting, characters, problem, solution); and
- can understand different points of view.

Here are some **activities** you can do during and after reading this book:
- Nonfiction: Nonfiction books deal with facts and events that are real. Discuss some of the facts you learned about Amelia Earhart.
- -ed Endings: List all the words in the story that have an -ed ending. On a separate piece of paper, write the root word next to the word with the -ed ending. The chart below will get you started:

word with an -ed ending	root word
loved	love
wanted	want
played	play

Remember, sharing the love of reading with a child is the best gift you can give!

—Sarah Fabiny, Editorial Director
   Penguin Young Readers program

*Penguin Young Readers are leveled by independent reviewers applying the standards developed by Irene Fountas and Gay Su Pinnell in *Matching Books to Readers: Using Leveled Books in Guided Reading*, Heinemann, 1999.

For Janet, who has Amelia's adventurous
spirit—BL

To my Grandpa, for showing me that adversity
can be overcome—JT

PENGUIN YOUNG READERS
An Imprint of Penguin Random House LLC

Penguin supports copyright. Copyright fuels creativity, encourages diverse voices, promotes free
speech, and creates a vibrant culture. Thank you for buying an authorized edition of this book
and for complying with copyright laws by not reproducing, scanning, or distributing any part of it
in any form without permission. You are supporting writers and allowing Penguin to continue to
publish books for every reader.

Text copyright © 2016 by Barbara Lowell. Illustrations copyright © 2016 by Jez Tuya. All rights reserved.
Published by Penguin Young Readers, an imprint of Penguin Random House LLC, 345 Hudson Street,
New York, New York 10014. Manufactured in China.

Library of Congress Cataloging-in-Publication Data is available.

ISBN 9780448487601 (pbk)   10 9 8 7 6 5 4 3 2 1
ISBN 9780448487618 (hc)   10 9 8 7 6 5 4 3 2 1

Daring Amelia

by Barbara Lowell
illustrated by Jez Tuya

Penguin Young Readers
An Imprint of Penguin Random House

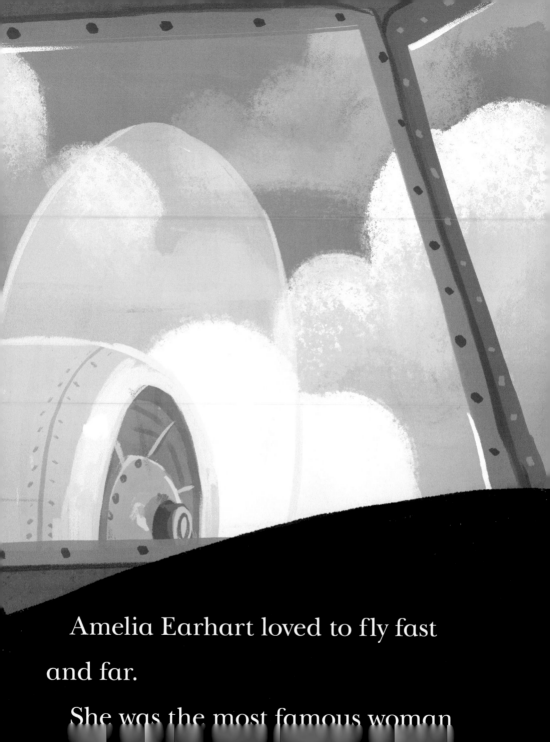

Amelia Earhart loved to fly fast and far.

She was the most famous woman

Amelia was born in Kansas
on July 24, 1897.

From the start, Amelia was
different than other girls.

She wanted to have adventures
like boys had.

Amelia rode a pony bareback.

She played baseball and
basketball.

She had mud-ball fights and
explored caves.

Lucky for Amelia, her parents
didn't mind.

Until Amelia built a roller coaster
in her backyard!

She sped down the track and crashed.

But daring Amelia loved the ride. She said, "It's just like flying."

When she was 20, Amelia moved
to Canada.

She worked as a nurse's aide,
caring for wounded soldiers.

There was an airfield nearby.

Amelia liked the stories the daring
pilots told her about flying.

One day, Amelia and a friend watched a pilot do tricks, called stunts.

The pilot flew right over them.

Amelia's friend ran away from the plane.

But Amelia liked what she saw.

She waved to the pilot.

Amelia wished she could fly, too.

In 1920, Amelia moved to
California to live with her parents.

She went to an air show with her
father.

The pilots raced and did stunts.
Amelia loved it.

"Dad, you know, I think I'd like
to fly," she said.

Her father asked a pilot if he
would take Amelia flying.

Amelia went for her first airplane ride the next day.

She saw the ocean and the Hollywood Hills.

From high above, they felt like new friends to her.

Now Amelia knew she had to learn to fly.

Amelia found a job to pay for flying lessons.

To look like other pilots, Amelia cut her hair very short. And she wore pants, boots, and a leather coat.

Amelia flew with her teacher, a woman pilot.

She learned to take off, make turns, and land.

Amelia loved flying.

After six months of lessons, she wanted her own plane.

With help from her mother, she could buy one.

Amelia bought a yellow plane,
small and fast. She named it
The Canary.

Soon, she had a new teacher.
He liked to do stunts.

Amelia learned to do stunts, too.

She did dives and rolls and spins.

And for the first time, she flew alone.

Daring Amelia was ready to take
off on her own adventures.

She was now one of the first
women pilots.

Amelia wanted to fly faster and
higher than anyone.

She flew in air shows, doing stunts.
One day, she flew higher than any
woman had ever flown before.

But then, in 1924, Amelia's parents divorced.

Amelia sold her plane to buy a car. Then she and her mother drove to Boston, their new home.

Amelia didn't forget about flying. In Boston, she made friends with pilots and flew in their planes.

In 1927, a man named Charles
Lindbergh did something daring.

He flew across the Atlantic Ocean
alone.

No one had done that before.

Charles Lindbergh wrote a book about his flight.

Then the publisher of the book had an idea.

He asked Amelia to be the first woman to fly across the Atlantic.

A man named Bill Stultz would fly the plane.

Amelia wasn't ready yet for such a long flight.

Slim Gordon, an airplane mechanic, would go, too.

Amelia would be the captain.

It was 1928, and the trip would be dangerous.

There were no instruments to help pilots see their location in bad weather.

Amelia wasn't afraid.

She thought it would be a daring adventure.

The name of the plane was *Friendship*.

The plane took off from and landed in the water.

Amelia liked its bright gold wings.

On June 17, 1928, *Friendship* took off.

The plane flew into fog and clouds.
Amelia and the men couldn't see
where they were going.

They used their radio to call ships.
People on the ships would tell them.

Then the radio broke.

They flew for hours and hours.

Were they still going the right way?
They didn't know.

With one hour of gas left, they had
to find out.

The pilot flew under the clouds and spotted a ship.

They could land near the ship, but then Amelia would not have crossed the ocean.

They kept going.

They were almost out of gas.

Finally, they landed.

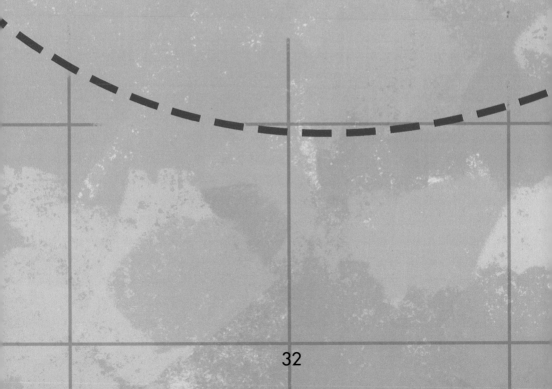

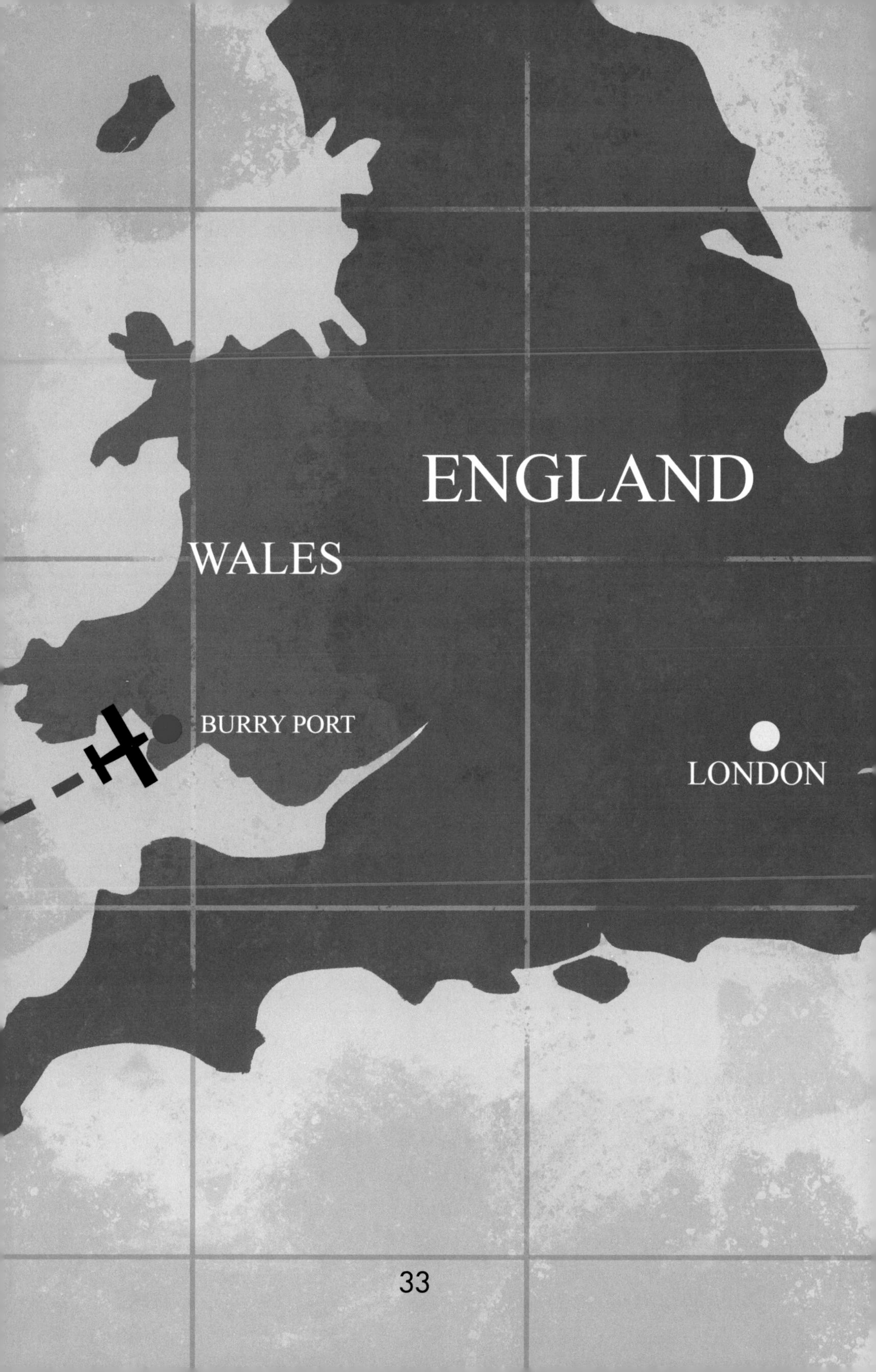

ENGLAND

WALES

BURRY PORT

LONDON

Everyone read the news.

"AMELIA EARHART CROSSES THE ATLANTIC!"

Amelia was famous.

She rode in a big parade in New York City.

She wrote a book about her
adventure.

But Amelia wanted something more.
She wanted to be the first woman to
fly across the Atlantic Ocean alone.

Soon, there were instruments to help pilots see. They wouldn't have to look out the window.

Amelia had the instruments put in her new plane.

She learned to fly using just the instruments.

This would help her if she flew into fog or rain.

On May 20, 1932, Amelia took off
on her solo flight.

She was going to fly all the way
to Paris.

One of Amelia's instruments showed
her how far above the ocean she was.

Then it stopped working.

Amelia flew into rain and then ice. Ice on a plane's wings could make it crash.

She had to fly closer to the ocean to melt the ice.

Amelia had to be careful not to fly too close to the ocean.

Sometimes she could see the waves.

Sometimes she had to guess how high up she was.

Hours went by.

Amelia wasn't sure where she was.

Amelia wanted to find land now.

She wouldn't fly all the way to Paris.

She spotted a fishing boat and knew she was close.

Then Amelia saw land.

It was Ireland.

She flew onto a field, surprising a farmer and his cows.

Amelia had done it!

She was the first woman to fly across the Atlantic Ocean alone.

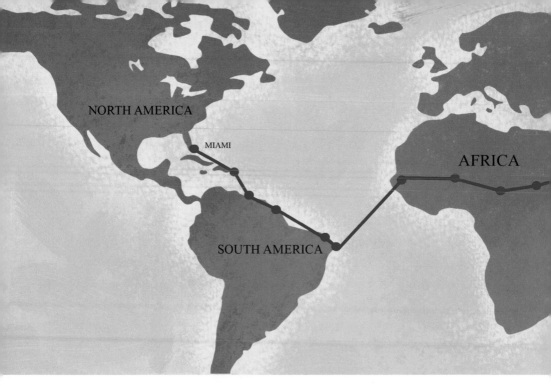

Now Amelia wanted to fly around the world.

No one had ever flown around the middle, called the equator.

Amelia bought a great big plane.

She took off from Miami, Florida, on June 1, 1937.

Fred Noonan, a navigator, went with her.

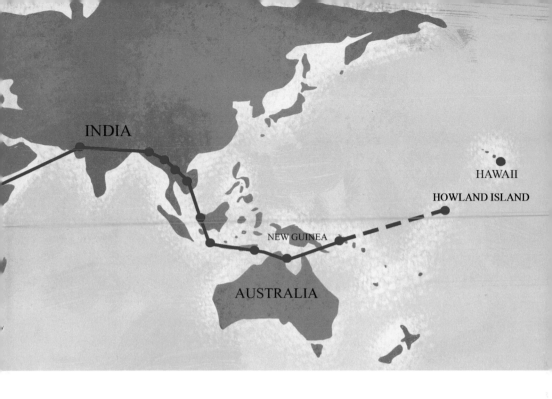

He looked at maps and the sun, moon, and stars to tell where they were.

Amelia stopped in many places. In South America, in Africa, in Australia.

People everywhere were happy to see her.

Then came the hardest part
of her trip.

Amelia had to land on a small
island. It was only a dot in the big
ocean.

She couldn't find it.

Daring Amelia was lost somewhere
in the Pacific Ocean.

Ships and planes looked for her.
She was never found.

THE CHRONICLE

BOS

EARHART M

EAR

GUARDIAN GAZETTE

FAINT S
HEARD

MISS

Amelia Earhart loved to fly.

That's the way people remember her.

Flying fast.

Flying far.